HIS STORY

(Volume 2)

A Simple Look Through

THE GOSPELS

Carmel Carberry
www.gardenlandministries.org
https://carmelcarberry.wordpress.com

Copyright © 2021 Carmel Carberry. All rights reserved.
This book is updated from the authors original work in 2019
Produced by Amazon Digital Services
ISBN: 9798739371935

Images by John and Carmel Carberry, and Georgie Carberry.
Special thanks to Ruth Irwin for cover photo.
Used with permission. All rights reserved.

Unless otherwise indicated, all Scripture quotations are taken from *the Holy Bible*, New Living Translation, copyright 1996, 2004. Used by permission of Tyndale House Publishers Inc., Wheaton, Illinois. All rights reserved.

Other Scripture quotations taken from the following versions of the *Holy Bible*:

New International Version (NIV) ~ *Holy Bible, New International Version®, NIV® Copyright © 1973, 1978, 1984, 2011 by Biblica, Inc.® Used by permission. All rights reserved worldwide*

The Message (MSG) ~ *Copyright © 1993, 1994, 1995, 1996, 2000, 2001, 2002 by Eugene H. Peterson*

Amplified Bible (AMP) ~ *Copyright © 1954, 1958, 1962, 1964, 1965, 1987 by The Lockman Foundation*

King James Version (KJV) ~ *By Public Domain*

New King James Version (NKJV) ~ *The Holy Bible, New King James Version Copyright © 1982 by Thomas Nelson, Inc.*

Good News Translation (GNT) ~ *Copyright © 1992 by American Bible Society*

New Life Version (NLV) ~ *Copyright © 1969 by Christian Literature International*

New Century Version (NCV) ~ *Copyright © 2005 by Thomas Nelson, Inc.*

Author's Note

Over the years, many people have told me that they find The Bible difficult to read, and that often they do not understand it. Yet there is such wonderful wisdom and wise counsel within its pages.

With this in mind, I hope that this series will help readers to understand a bit more from the wealth of knowledge that The Scriptures contain and begin to enjoy them.

I pray that this insight helps readers to know deeper The One whom The Bible points to: The God of Love who is seen through His Son Jesus, who came for you.

you hold a special

place in Gods heart

You are dearly loved by
God The Father
and held secure
in Jesus

CONTENTS

SIMPLE OVERVIEW OF THE BIBLE   Page 1

Section 1   Introduction (The Gospels)   Page 7

Section 2   The Saviour is Born   Page 15

Section 3   Teaching and Parables   Page 27

Section 4   Healings and Miracles   Page 39

Section 5   The Cross   Page 47

Section 6   Jesus is Alive!   Page 59

Section 7   The Holy Spirit   Page 69

Personal study notes   Page 75

About The Author and 'Gardenland'   Page 87

Encouragements and Prayer   Page 91

ENCOURAGEMENT
FROM GOD'S HEART

*I AM with you ~ fear not, for I AM here.
I give you My Rose of Love ~ Jesus Christ,
God personified for you.*

*There are no thorns upon My Rose of Love,
no rejection, no condemnation.*

*I give you My heart, My strength and My joy,
not as the world gives, for I give peace
that is far greater.*

*My power is strong but full of grace
and gentleness for you.*

*I welcome you, love you, accept you, so let
your heart rest in the everlasting arms that
surround you day after day, and for all eternity.*

*I have given you My Son ~ My life, My heart,
you have everything you need in Him.*

SIMPLE OVERVIEW OF THE BIBLE

The OLD TESTAMENT consists of the first 39 books of The Bible. The name 'Testament' refers to a covenant (meaning a 'binding agreement' or 'promise') that has been made between God and man.

In the Old Testament, we see that God made promises to men of faith who lived long ago; and God remains faithful to His promises *(for example: Adam ~ Genesis 1:26-30 // Noah ~ Genesis 9:11 // Abraham ~ Genesis 12:1-3 // Moses ~ Exodus 19-24 // David ~ 2 Samuel 5:7)*

The Bible begins by telling us that God is the Creator of all life and the whole universe. It introduces us to the first human beings and their descendants, with an emphasis on Abraham, his son Isaac, and his grandson Jacob.... who fathered the nation Israel.

Then the story of the Israelites' exodus from Egypt is told, and the development of Israel as a nation, including a variety of laws that were given to them.

There are also accounts of Leaders and Kings who ruled over the people and the many up and downs that this small but enduring nation faced over the centuries.

God spoke through many prophets to this nation with guidance, encouragements, and warnings, but also gave a message for the whole world through them that He would send an eternal Saviour who would come for all mankind.

The Bible as a whole shows mankind's need for a Saviour, and it prophesies about Him throughout the Old Testament.

Many rituals in the Old Testament (OT) have symbolism attached to them that act as a pointer towards the promised 'Christ' *(meaning 'Anointed One')*. Many of the Biblical heroes are also like 'types' or 'shadows' that point to Him.

Jesus is The Christ who is revealed in the New Testament (NT).
Some Bible references to consider: Isaiah 9:6 (OT) //
Matthew 1:23 / Matt 22:36-40 / Rom 10:4 (NT)

The NEW TESTAMENT is composed of the remaining 27 books of The Bible.

As we saw previously, the name 'Testament' refers to a covenant (agreement or promise) made between God and man. Ultimately, the fulfilment of all the Old Testament laws and prophets has come through Jesus *(Matt 5:17)*.

The New Testament shows us the NEW COVENANT, which is the Eternal Covenant of Grace that God has made through the complete and finished work of Jesus at The Cross, and by His Resurrection *(Rom 3:23-26 / Heb 1:1-3)*.

The New Testament tells us how Jesus accomplished salvation for all mankind and showed us God's Heart *(John 1:18)*. We see the Love and Grace of God revealed in His Life and Ministry, as shown in The Gospels (Matthew, Mark, Luke, and John).

Then the New Testament pages tell us about the pouring out of God's Holy Spirit, the growth and impact of the early church (Acts) and records letters written by The Apostles to encourage and instruct the early church, and the generations that followed.

We can glean great wisdom, encouragement and insight through all of these, which lead us to 'Good News' ~ The Revelation of God's Love and Grace through Christ, God's One and Only Son *(John 3:16-17)*

The following pages list the names of the 66 books that make up the Bible as we know it. Then, some verses from the Gospel of John (John1:1-18) are shared (taken from the 'New Life Version' of The Bible).

This is followed by sections one to six which offer a simple look through The Gospels (Matthew, Mark, Luke, John) in a chronological order of events. Bible references are given in each section for further study if desired.

Bible Books Overview

Old Testament book titles with brief, simplistic description

- GENESIS – Creation, Noah, Tower of Babel, Abraham, Isaac, Jacob; Joseph and the beginning of the nation Israel
- EXODUS – Israel escape from Egypt after being held in slavery
- LEVITICUS – The Law of Moses is given to Israel
- NUMBERS – Israel wanders through the desert
- DEUTERONOMY – a continued history of Israel
- JOSHUA – an account of Israel entering the Promised Land
- JUDGES – a time of no clear leadership (inc. story of Samson)
- RUTH – a story of romance and family loyalty
- 1&2 SAMUEL – the first Kings of Israel (inc. King David)
- 1&2 KINGS – stories of success and failure
- 1&2 CHRONICLES – a history of David's royal line
- EZRA – the nation returns to the land God promised
- NEHEMIAH – the rebuilding of Jerusalem
- ESTHER – a queen acts bravely to save her people
- JOB – a man is restored after a time of suffering
- PSALMS – poems and songs, written and sung for God
- PROVERBS – wise advice (generally from Solomon)
- ECCLESIASTES – life is meaningless without God
- SONG OF SONGS – a story of adoring love
- ISAIAH – warnings; future hope; promises of a Saviour
- JEREMIAH – God is on The Throne, despite bad times
- LAMENTATIONS – a nation recalls their suffering
- EZEKIEL – visions of heaven; messages to nations
- DANIEL – a story of faith through difficult times
- HOSEA – a story of disloyalty
- JOEL – mercy triumphs over judgement
- AMOS – a call for justice
- OBADIAH – God defeats His enemies

- JONAH – God's message delivers a city
- MICAH – a crisis followed by hope
- NAHUM – God is to be honoured
- HABAKKUK – life doesn't always make sense
- ZEPHANIAH – the day of God's promise is near
- HAGGAI – a call to get ready
- ZECHARIAH – promises of restoration
- MALACHI – the promised Saviour is coming

New Testament book titles with a brief, simplistic description

- The Gospel of MATTHEW – Looking at Jesus: The Saviour is here!
- The Gospel of MARK – Looking at Jesus: Healer and Deliverer
- The Gospel of LUKE – Looking at Jesus: He came for all people
- The Gospel of JOHN – Looking at Jesus: God is with us
- ACTS – Christ ascends to heaven; the Holy Spirit is poured out on all flesh; Jesus' message of God's mercy begins to be proclaimed to all the earth
- ROMANS – Christ, the hope of all nations
- 1&2 CORINTHIANS – instruction on how to confront problems
- GALATIANS – Christ has set you free, stay free!
- EPHESIANS – a picture of who we are in Christ
- PHILIPPIANS – instruction to follow the example of Jesus
- COLOSSIANS – a description of the completeness of Jesus
- 1&2 THESSALONIANS – encouragement for today and forever
- 1&2 TIMOTHY – instruction on how to manage a difficult task
- TITUS – encouragement to finish the job
- PHILEMON – encouragement to forgive a fellow believer
- HEBREWS – the message of the New Covenant, sealed by Jesus
- JAMES – instruction on how to live a life of faith
- 1&2 PETER – encouragement to keep believing
- 1&2&3 JOHN – stay focused on God's love and truth
- JUDE – encouragement to stay in faith
- REVELATION – A vision of The Heavenly King Jesus; a look at world events from Heaven's perspective; a promise that God is making all things new!

John Chapter 1:1-18 (NLV)

¹ The Word (Christ) was in the beginning. The Word was with God. The Word was God. ² He was with God in the beginning. ³ He made all things. Nothing was made without Him making it. ⁴ Life began by Him. His Life was the Light for men. ⁵ The Light shines in the darkness. The darkness has never been able to put out the Light.

⁶ There was a man sent from God whose name was John. ⁷ He came to tell what he knew about the Light so that all men might believe through him. ⁸ John was not the Light, but he was sent to tell about the Light.

⁹ This true Light, coming into the world, gives light to every man. ¹⁰ He came into the world. The world was made by Him, but it did not know Him. ¹¹ He came to His own, but His own did not receive Him. ¹² He gave the right and the power to become children of God to those who received Him. He gave this to those who put their trust in His name.

¹³ These children of God were not born of blood and of flesh and of man's desires, but they were born of God. ¹⁴ Christ became human flesh and lived among us. We saw His shining-greatness. This greatness is given only to a much-loved Son from His Father. He was full of loving-favour and truth.

¹⁵ John told about Christ and said, "I have been telling you about this One. I said, 'He is coming after me. He is more important than I because He lived before me.'" ¹⁶ From Him Who has so much we have all received loving-favor, one loving-favor after another.

¹⁷ The Law was given through Moses, but loving-favor and truth came through Jesus Christ. ¹⁸ The much-loved Son is beside the Father. No man has ever seen God. But Christ has made God known to us.

INTRODUCTION

Introducing The Gospels

The word 'Gospel' means 'Good News'. The first four books of The New Testament (Matthew, Mark, Luke and John) tell the reader about the ***Good News of Jesus***.

The four Gospels look at His birth, life, ministry, death and resurrection. Each book is written from a different perspective by its writer.

They are like newspaper reports speaking from the perspective of four witnesses' observations of an event.

When each account is considered alongside the others, it builds a clearer picture of The Person of Christ and the true Heart of God, which is seen through Jesus.

Each account speaks of the divinity of Jesus (Matt 1:23, Matt 3:13-17, Mark 1:1, Mark 1:9-11, Luke 1:32-35, Luke 3:21-22, Luke 4:18-21, John 1:1, John 1:29-34)

They all record Jesus helping people, for example through healings, miracles and powerful teaching (Matt 4-25, Mark 1-13, Luke 4-19, John 2-17).

They all tell about the events of The Cross, where Jesus died to pay for the sin of all mankind (Matt 26-27, Mark 14-15, Luke 19:28-23:56, John 18-19).

They all delight in the resurrection of Christ, declaring that He is alive forever, and He is with us always (Matt 28, Mark 16, Luke 24, John 20).

Generally speaking, scholars consider that The Gospels were written approximately 50-100 AD.

In the Gospel of John, the writer informs us that the ministry of Jesus is so abundant, that the world cannot hold enough books to fully tell of all the great things He has done!

However, John also tells us the reason that we have The Gospels (and indeed the whole Bible) is so that we can learn and know about The One who has come to give us Eternal Life in His Name.

John 21:25 / John 20:31 (KJV)
...there are many other things which Jesus did, the which, if they should be written every one, I suppose that even the world itself could not contain the books that should be written.... But these are written so that you may believe that Jesus is the Messiah, the Son of God, and that by believing you may have Life in His Name.

Writers Aims and Themes

MATTHEW

As a man from Israel, Matthew knew about Jewish Law, beliefs and customs. As he wrote The Gospel of Matthew, he could relate to these and draw on them to express the message he wanted to convey.

Jewish readers would be able to relate to many of the points he makes in his account, which was likely his aim.

Matthew's writing begins with a reference to Genesis 2:4 (of the Old Testament) ~ using the words 'The Book of Genealogy' (which means 'Genesis' in Greek) of Jesus Christ.

Matthew identifies Jesus as the 'Son of David' (referring to King David of Israel's history) with a lineage that can be traced back to Abraham.

As he continues to write, he frequently refers to Old Testament prophesies to offer his witness that Jesus was (and is) The Messiah, whom the Jews were looking for.

With this in mind, his aim appears to be to help his readers understand that Jesus fulfilled 'The Law and The Prophets' (as found in The Old Testament) in all their fullness, confirming that Jesus is everything He claimed to be.

Note:
Son of David *was an Old Testament title that referred to the promised* **Saviour / Messiah** *~ who would come from the family line of King David (who himself was a descendant of Abraham)*

MARK

It is understood that The Gospel of Mark was written by a man called 'John Mark' who is mentioned in Acts 12:12.

John was the writer's Hebrew name; and Mark was the writer's Latin name. Thus, we see other Bible references speaking of this man using the name 'John Mark'.

Many believe that John Mark was a pupil/student of Peter's, to whom Peter told his personal stories of being with Jesus. John Mark wrote these down, and these writings became The Gospel of Mark that we know today.

The original intended audience appears to have been the Greek-speaking people of the time (who were part of The Roman Empire). These people were known as 'gentiles' (non-Jews).

The aim of the writing was to offer an account that could be understood by those who did not have a background understanding of Old Testament scripture, rituals and Law.

So, Mark writes an action-packed Gospel, including Jesus performing miracles, to show that He had supernatural power. But the greatest focus is the 'Passion of Christ' (Jesus' death followed by His Resurrection).

Mark devotes most of his writing to the events of The Cross, to declare that Jesus has conquered both sin and death, which is the greatest miracle of all.

Mark concludes with the Ascension of Christ (into Heaven) after Jesus had spoken with His disciples, commissioning them and promising that He will be with them always.

Mark 16:19-20 (GNT)
After the Lord Jesus had talked with them, He was taken up to heaven and sat at the right side of God. The disciples went and preached everywhere, and the Lord worked with them and proved that their preaching was true by the miracles that were performed.

LUKE

Luke is understood to have been a doctor (as mentioned in Colossians 4:14) and a companion of The Apostle Paul. As well as his Gospel account, Luke also recorded the 'Book of Acts' ~ which follows The Gospels in the New Testament (Luke 1:1-4 / Acts 1:1-2).

Note:
'ACTS' describes how the Holy Spirit worked in and through the lives of many of Jesus' followers after He had returned to Heaven. It introduces us to The Apostle Paul, tells about the birth and life of The Early Church, and how Jesus followers took the Good News about Him around the world. It also shows us how Jesus remains active in the lives of all who trust in Him.

Both the Gospel of Luke, and the Book of Acts, appear to have been written to give a record of events to a man named 'Theophilus'. This man is believed to have been the defence lawyer for Paul.

Luke was gathering evidence for Theophilus to use in his defence of Paul. Luke also states at the beginning of his writing that he has made his own investigations, and that he wants to give testimony concerning 'The Word' (a reference to Jesus ~ Luke 1:3 / John 1:1)

Luke writes in a way that can be read by anyone, and encourages the reader in the love and grace of God, to know Him more, through His Son, Jesus.

Luke 1:1-4 (NIV)
Many have undertaken to draw up an account of the things that have been fulfilled among us, just as they were handed down to us by those who from the first were eyewitnesses and servants of The Word. With this in mind, since I myself have carefully investigated everything from the beginning, I too decided to write an orderly account for you, most excellent Theophilus, so that you may know the certainty of the things you have been taught.

JOHN

John was one of Jesus' disciples and understood the love that Jesus had for people, including him personally. So, he often used the phrase 'the disciple Jesus loved' in his Gospel.

John also wrote the 'Book of Revelation' and three of the New Testament Letters (1 John, 2 John and 3 John) to share more revelation about the Person of Christ.

The first chapter of The Gospel of John refers to Jesus as ***The Word*** (***logos***), declaring that The Word has always existed and was involved in Creation itself. The Ancient Greek's used the term *'logos'* to refer to *'**the principle of cosmic reason**'*. It was also similar in context to the Hebrew idea of '***Wisdom***'.

John writes about Jesus in this context, being the source of all life and the creator of all things. His use of phrases that seem obscure to us today would have had great meaning during the time they were written.

With that understanding, John's Gospel can offer the reader great insight and begin to answer questions, such as "Who is Jesus?" "What was He like?" "Did He make everything?" "Is He really God?"

John 1:1-3+14+18 (NIV)
*In the beginning was the Word, and **the Word was with God, and the Word was God**. He was with God in the beginning. Through Him all things were made; without Him nothing was made that has been made....*
The Word became flesh and made His dwelling among us. *We have seen His glory, the glory of the one and only Son, who came from the Father, full of grace and truth....*
*No one has ever seen God, but **the one and only Son, who is Himself God** and is in closest relationship with the Father, has made Him known.*

When the great insight of all Four Gospels is put together, there is so much to see and learn from them. Individually and collectively they encourage and bless the reader in the Love and Grace of God Himself, which seen in its fullness in His Son, who holds all things together. It's His Story.

Taken from Hebrews 1:1-3 (NIV)
*In the past God spoke...at many times and in various ways, but in these last days **He has spoken to us by His Son… through whom He made the universe.... The Son is the radiance of God's glory and the exact representation of His being,** sustaining all things by His powerful word.*

Section Two

The Saviour is Born

USING INFORMATION TAKEN FROM THE GOSPELS AND
BRINGING IT TOGETHER, THIS SECTION WILL SHARE
A SIMPLE OVERVIEW OF THE BIRTH AND LIFE OF JESUS.

The Word becomes a human being

Before all time, Jesus existed. God *'spoke'* all creation into being through His *'Eternal Word'* (Jesus, His Son). Jesus is God's *'Everlasting Light'* who shines for all mankind.

His Light came into the world in the form of a human being: **God Himself visited mankind upon the earth in the Person of His Son.**

God's Light appeared to a nation who had a history of men and women that had put their trust in God, even though they had not seen Him; they heard about Him and believed.

The Light was born as a human being (into a human family) from the historical line of a man named Abraham. The descendants of Abraham had grown into a small but resilient nation, whom God had spoken to across the ages.

God wanted to speak through this nation (called 'Israel') to speak to all nations; therefore He sent His Son into this genetic line to make Himself known to all people.

The Birth of John The Baptist

A man named Zacharias (who was one of the nation's priests) and his wife Elizabeth, had long wanted to have a child but Elizabeth was not able to have children.

In their old age, an angel appeared to Zacharias with a message from God, promising that his wife would have a child despite the odds against them.

Initially the priest was filled with unbelief and could not speak. Elizabeth became pregnant, and when the child was born, Zacharias' speech returned, and he named the child 'John' (which means 'God is gracious') ~ *the child John later became known as 'John The Baptist.*

Mary and Joseph

During the time Elizabeth was pregnant with her child John, an angel also appeared to her cousin Mary, to tell her that God's Spirit would bring about the supernatural conception of a child in her womb and that she was to name Him '***Jesus***' (which means '***Saviour***').

Mary believed God's Word, then went to visit her cousin with the good news. The moment Elisabeth and Mary met, 'John' (while still in his mother's womb) jumped for joy, and the two women rejoiced together and praised God.

An angel also spoke to the man that Mary was engaged to marry, Joseph, to reassure him to take Mary as his wife and to bring up the child she carried, and be a family. Joseph was a man of honour and integrity, so he obeyed God and took care of Mary and her child.

The Roman Emperor of the time ordered that a census be taken in Israel, which required all citizens to return to their home town to register.

Therefore, while Mary was still pregnant, Mary and Joseph travelled to Bethlehem to register for this census. After several days of travel, Mary and Joseph arrived in Bethlehem, searching for a place to stay.

The Birth of Jesus

At Bethlehem, all the Inns were full, but one Innkeeper (on seeing that Mary was due to give birth soon) told Joseph that they could stay in his stable instead.

So, they settled down for the night alongside the animals. Mary went into labour and gave birth to Jesus in the stable. They made a bed for him in an animals feeding trough (known as a manger).

About this time, an angel appeared to some shepherds who were keeping watch over some sheep in the fields near Bethlehem. The angel told the shepherds that the Saviour had been born and told them where to find Him, to go and honour Him.

Then a chorus of angels appeared and sang praises to God. So, the shepherds went to find the baby laying in the manger (just as the angel has said) and worshipped Him.

After some time, some wise men (also known as 'The Magi') saw a magnificent star that had rested over the place where Jesus lay.

These 'wise men' (also known as 'Stargazers' or 'Astronomers') travelled from a far eastern country to find the new born king.

On their way, the wise men met with Herod (the King of Judah at that time). Herod told the men to come back and tell him where the baby was. But Herod's intention was not as he said (to 'worship the child') but to kill the child.

The Wise Men followed the Great Star and found the child. They worshipped Him and gave gifts of gold, frankincense and myrrh. But they travelled back to their home country by a different route to avoid Herod, recognizing his real intentions.

Dedication at the Temple

The religious practice of the land was to take the first boy child of a family to The Temple at Jerusalem, where the parents would make an offering of thanks to God.

So, when Jesus was 40 days old, Mary and Joseph took Him to The Temple and brought a pair of young pigeons to be their offering.

There was a man in Jerusalem named Simeon (a man who had dedicated his life to God). He was now very old but was resting on the promise that God gave him from years before that he would not die before seeing The Saviour.

One day, Simeon felt The Holy Spirit's prompting to go to The Temple. So, he went and was there when Joseph and Mary came in with Jesus to present their offering.

When Simeon saw the child, God spoke to him to tell him that this was (is) the promised Saviour.

With great rejoicing, Simeon took Jesus in his arms and blessed Him, gave thanks for Him, and thanked God for letting Simeon see 'The Christ' as He had promised. Simeon also blessed Mary and Joseph, and prophesied of things to come.

Simeon told Mary of great things that her child would do but also warned her that 'sorrow would pierce her heart like a sword' (this was a reference to The Cross).

At the same time, a woman named Anna was also in The Temple (she too had dedicated her life to God, and spent much of her time praying).

The Holy Spirit revealed to her too that the child was The Saviour, so she gave thanks to God and she told others in The Temple that The Redeemer had come.

A Time of Horror

When Herod learned that the Wise Men had returned to their home country without reporting back to him, he began plotting again to try and kill the child (knowing He was special).

Herod was afraid that the potential popularity of this child could become a threat to his ruling of the land and so he became jealous. In his rage and evil thoughts, Herod gave orders to have all the children in Bethlehem killed, who were two years old and under.

A Time of Rescue

But God spoke to Joseph in a dream to warn him to take his family to Egypt where Herod had no authority in the land. So Joseph, Mary and Jesus fled to Egypt and stayed there until Herod died.

After Herod's passing, the family set out for Bethlehem again. However, when they discovered that Herod's son had taken control of that part of Israel, they decided instead to go back to Nazareth (the town where Mary grew up), in the northern part of Israel (in Galilee).

Jesus Childhood

In Galilee, Jesus spent His childhood working alongside Joseph as a carpenter. Jesus grew up like any normal child, except that he demonstrated great wisdom and understanding beyond human expectation. His incredible knowledge amazed great scholars and teachers who had studied religious scriptures all of their lives.

Every year, Mary and Joseph would go to Jerusalem (along with their family and relatives) to celebrate The Passover. *(The Passover is an annual Jewish festival, which celebrates the release of the Israelites from slavery in Egypt, as recorded in The Old Testament).*

When Jesus was only 12 years old, he stayed behind in Jerusalem on one of these occasions to talk with The Scribes and Pharisees (who were long standing Teachers of Religious Law).

When His parents came searching for Him, they found Jesus in The Temple of Jerusalem, in full debate with the Religious Leaders. Jesus spoke with great insight and spiritual truth as He talked with them.

The Religious Leaders were amazed at His understanding and His depth of knowledge of The Scriptures, and He referred to them as though they came from His heart.

John Begins to Preach and Baptise

After some years, the son of Zachariah and Elizabeth (John) went out to live in the wilderness and began preaching and prophesying about The Promised Saviour.

The people of Jerusalem and the whole Judean countryside went out to listen to him as he cried out to people to turn to God and then baptised them in the River Jordan. Thus, he became known as 'John The Baptist'.

Jesus' Baptism

One day, Jesus came looking for John and requested to be baptised by him. His response to Jesus was: 'should I not be coming to you?' But Jesus told him that it was to fulfil God's will to do this, and so John baptised Jesus.

As He rose up from the water, God's Holy Spirit descended upon Jesus like a dove, and God The Father's voice spoke from heaven saying, 'This is My Son, with Whom I AM pleased'.

When Jesus went on His way, John pointed to Jesus and told the people watching: 'Behold The Lamb of God who takes way the sins of the world'. John said that Jesus was The One he had been prophesying about.

A Time of Temptation

From there, Jesus went in the wilderness and spent 40 days and nights where He fasted and was tempted by the devil. Jesus responded to every temptation and accusation by quoting The Scriptures and standing on the truth of God's Word throughout.

The Bible tells us that during Jesus life, He was tempted in every way that each one of us are also tempted. But He was without sin. Therefore, He can relate to each one of us at our point of need, and help us to overcome.

Jesus came out of the wilderness in power and victory, and angels ministered to Him. After this, He began His public ministry (at 30 years old).

The Calling of Jesus' Disciples

Jesus called twelve ordinary people to become His disciples. He went about doing good and healing all who came to Him. Everywhere Jesus went He showed God's Love to people who did not deserve it ~ He showed them God's grace and mercy.

Thousands of people followed Him as He preached from place to place, teaching about God, performing miracles and healing people of all kinds of sickness and diseases.

The people saw a man who spoke with authority and demonstrated God's nature in the most powerful way they had ever seen.

His growing popularity among the people led to jealousy developing amongst some religious leaders, who saw their own personal status decline.

So, they sought to discredit Jesus and began to plot against Him. This resulted in a number of confrontations between the religious authorities and Jesus. However, Jesus could turn every situation around and speak more about God's Love at every occasion.

He never compromised God's Laws; He fulfilled each one in full. He called for people to believe in Him and to trust in God. He preached that salvation was a free gift from God Himself.

He also prophesied that He would pay the price for all sin, for all people, through His death on The Cross. But this appalled many who could not understand what He meant, and the disciples did not want to lose their Master, who they loved.

Jesus loved people so much that He determined to fulfil God's instruction to Him, which God had said was the only way to save mankind.

Despite persecution from religious authorities, Jesus ate and drank alongside people rejected by society. He showed mercy and grace to them and encouraged all to live a life that honored God. But Jesus never rejected anyone who came to Him in faith.

Jesus often confronted the demands of 'Religious Law' and those who put burdens on the people. He released people from spiritual oppression and taught people God's ways.

He knew that after The Cross, He would rise from the dead, and focused His Heart and Mind on the joy of seeing those who would come to Him, redeemed and set free.

So, He continued to perform healings and miracles among the people, and kept on speaking **His message of salvation for all who would believe in The Son.**

> *John 3:16-17 Amplified Bible (AMP)*
> *For God so [greatly] loved and dearly prized the world, that He [even] gave His [One and] only begotten Son, so that whoever believes and trusts in Him [as Saviour] shall not perish but have eternal life. For God did not send the Son into the world to judge and condemn the world [that is, to initiate the final judgment of the world], but that the world might be saved through Him.*

> *Matthew 22:36-40 (NIV) (Jesus was asked) ...*
> *"Teacher, which is the greatest commandment in the Law?" Jesus replied: "'Love the Lord your God with all your heart and with all your soul and with all your mind.' This is the first and greatest commandment. And the second is like it: 'Love your neighbour as yourself.' All the Law and the Prophets hang on these two commandments."*

RELATED BIBLE REFERENCES
FOR SOME KEY POINTS IN THIS PART OF HIS STORY

The Word becomes a human being (John 1:1-14)
The Angel Gabriel speaks to Mary (Luke 1:26-38)
Mary visits Elizabeth (Luke 1:39-45)
Mary's Song of Praise (Luke 1:46-55)
Birth of John The Baptist (Luke 1:5-25 / Luke 1:57-80)
Birth of Jesus (Matt 1:18-25 / Luke 2:1-39 / Matt 2:1-12)
Fleeing to Egypt / Persecution from Herod (Matt 2:13-18)
Returning to Nazareth (Matt 2:19-23 / Luke 2:39)
Jesus' Childhood and Visit to the Temple (Luke 2:40-52)
Preaching of John The Baptist (Matt 3:1-12 / Mark 1:1-8 /
/ Luke 3:10-14 / John 1:15-28)
The Baptism of Jesus (Matt 3:13-17 / Mark 1:9-11 / Luke 3:21-22)
John recognizes Jesus as the 'Lamb of God' (John 1:29-34)
Temptation of Christ (Matt 4:1-11 / Mark 1:12-13 / Luke 4:1-13)
Jesus Begins Preaching in Galilee
Matt 4:12-17 / Mark 1:14-15 / Luke 4:14-15+42-44
Matt 4:23-25 / Mark 1: 39-44 / Luke 6:17-19
Jesus calls His First Disciples
Matt 4:18-22 / Mark 1:16-20 / Luke 5:1-11 / John 1:35-51

Further reference lists of Jesus' 'Teaching & Parables' plus 'Healings & Miracles' can be found in the next sections, followed by the continuing of His Story leading to The Cross, Resurrection and Ascension of Christ.

Section Three

Teaching & Parables

Parables are short stories that teach a moral or spiritual lesson using something familiar to the reader / listener. The first century audience were most familiar with agricultural life.

Therefore, many of Jesus' parables were based around this theme and the way of life that those He was speaking to would have known and understood.

Much of Jesus' teaching was about The Kingdom of God and spiritual truths. We can learn more about our relationship with God as we consider the things He taught.

When we consider the parables of Jesus by using the understanding of the day, we can learn great insight from them. Applying these truths into our own lives (and world) today can help us walk in wisdom.

With this in mind, I have offered some thoughts on one of the parables (following the list of examples below). However, there is much more that I recommend for personal (and prayerful) study, whilst listening to God's Heart of Love and Grace.

~~~~~~~~~

EXAMPLES OF PARABLES AND SYMBOLISM
WHICH JESUS USED IN HIS TEACHING
(with Bible references for further study)

- **Salt and Light**
  Matt 5:13-16 / Matt 6:22-23 / Mark 9:49-50 / Luke 14:34-35

- **The Light of The Body**
  Matt 6:22-23 / Luke 11:34-36

- **Do not give Pearls to Swine**
  Matt 7:6

- **The Narrow Gate**
  Matt 7:13-14 / Matt 7:21-23 / Luke 13:22-30

- **By Their Fruits (you shall know them)**
  Matt 7:15-20 / Matt 12:33-37 / Luke 6:43-45

- **Building a House on Sand**
  Matt 7:24-28 / Luke 6:46-49

- **Sheep without a Shepherd**
  Matt 9:36-38

- **The Sower**
  Matt 13:1-9 / Mark 4:3-9 / Luke 8:4-8
  Matt 13:18-23 / Mark 4:13-20 / Luke 8:11-15

- **Light Under A Bushel**
  Mark 4:21-25 / Luke 8:16-18 / Luke 11:33

- **The Growing Seed**
  Mark 4:26-29

- **Wheat and Tares**
  Matt 13:24-30

- **The Mustard Seed**
  Matt 13:31-32 / Mark 4:30-32 / Luke 13:18-19

- **The Leaven**
  Matt 13:33 / Luke 13:20-21
  Matt 16:5-12 / Mark 8:14-21 / John 6:26-58

- **Pearl of Great Price**
  Matt 13:44-46

- **The Great Net**
  Matt 13:47-50

- **The True Bread of Life**
  John 6:26-58

- **Rivers of Living Waters**
  John 7:37-39

- **The Light of The World**
  John 8:12-20 / John 9:1-12

- **The Lost Sheep**
  Matt 18:11-14 / Luke 15:1-7

- **The Sheepfold**
  John 10:1-6

- **The Good Shepherd**
  John 10:7-21

- **An Unforgiving Servant**
  Matt 18:21-35

- **The Good Samaritan**
  Luke 10:25-37

- **A Rich Fool**
  Luke 12:13-21

- **The Barren Fig Tree**
  Luke 13:6-9

- **The Lost Coin**
  Luke 15:8-10

- **The Prodigal Son**
  Luke 15:11-32

- **The Shrewd Steward**
  Luke 16:1-12

- **Lazarus and The Rich Man**
  Luke 16:19-31

- **Faith as a Mustard Seed**
  Luke 17:5-10

- **The Widow and The Judge**
  Luke 18:1-8

- **The Pharisee and The Publican**
  Luke 18-9-14

- **The Labourers**
  Matt 20:1-16

- **The Talents**
  Matt 25:14-30 / Luke 19:11-27

- **The Grain of Wheat**
  John 12:24

- **The Light in The Darkness**
  John 12:46-47

- **Lesson of The Fig Tree**
  Matt 21:20-22 / Matt 24:32-35 /
  Mark 11:20-26 / Mark 13:28-31 / Luke 21:29-33

- **The Two Sons**
  Matt 21:28-32

- **The Wicked Husbandman**
  Matt 21:33-46 / Mark 12:1-12 / Luke 20:9-19

- **The Marriage Feast**
  Matt 22:1-14 / Luke 14:16-24

- **The True Vine**
  John 15:1-17

- **The Faithful Servant**
  Matt 24:45-51 / Luke 12:41-48

- **The Ten Virgins**
  Matt 25:1-13

~~~~~~~

SOME THOUGHTS TO CONSIDER:

Through the story of **The Parable of The Sower** Jesus shows how God's Kingdom works. Understanding this parable can help us understand the other things Jesus taught.

The Seed that the farmer is sowing represents **God's Word** and the ***different types of ground*** are representative of ***people's hearts***. Jesus' parable is showing how the **Promises of God** can be sown (like a seed) into our hearts.

The seed that fell on the footpath shows that when we do not understand God's Word, it has difficulty taking root and making the changes to our lives that it could if it was fully received and understood.

The path can also represent a heart that refuses to receive the truth of The Word. Then the wonderful truths that could change lives are simply lost or neglected.

However, good teaching and clear explanations can be a great help to us to gain real understanding, along with keeping our hearts tender towards God (to help ourselves listen to what He is saying to us at any time).

The rocky ground shows what can happen when we are quick to receive God's Word, but we do not take time to nurture the truths learned. Unfortunately, in this instance, roots would not have time to develop and grow.

Thus, when times are difficult, the growth of the seed can be easily disturbed by the 'storms of life' that we all encounter at some point. But God will always help us as we turn to Him in faith. He will show us how to put our roots deep into Him.

The thorny ground shows what happens when we receive God's Word but the cares and worries of this life (represented by the thorns and weeds) begin to choke the roots and hinder the growth of God's Word inside our hearts.

His Word could have produced great results, but it can be hampered from doing so when we keep our hearts and minds focused too much on life's cares and worries, therefore despite growth, fruit does not develop.

It's important to remember that: ***the way we think determines our actions and our corresponding feelings***

Taken from Proverbs 23:7 (KJV)
For as (a person) thinks in his heart, so is he.

Therefore, it is good to think upon and consider what God says about the situations we find ourselves in, and make conscious choices to trust Him despite circumstances, or negative thoughts and emotions.

The good soil shows what can happen when we receive God's Word and allow it to grow deep inside our hearts. As we keep our minds and hearts fixed on Him, the seed can grow roots and with room to grow unhindered, it ultimately produces a harvest of good things for us.

By learning more about God's Grace and Mercy, we can begin to see that He loves ALL people everywhere and is calling ALL to repentance and faith in Jesus. He is good, and no one is rejected by Him, but we all have a choice whether to receive or reject His Love.

God's Everlasting Arms are open wide towards us.

~~~~~~~~

SOME MORE EXAMPLES OF JESUS TEACHING
(with Bible references for further study)

- **Jesus Teaches with Authority**
  Mark 1:21-28 / Luke 4:31-37

- **Being Born of The Spirit**
  John 3:1-21

- **Sermon on The Mount**
  For full sermon, see Matthew chapters 5, 6 and 7

- **The Beatitudes** *(sometimes known as 'Beautiful Attitudes')*
  Matt 5:3-12 / Luke 6:20-23

- **Jesus came to Fulfil The Law**
  Matt 5:17-20

- **Love Your Enemies / Bless Do Not Curse**
  Matt 5:43-48 / Matt 7:12 / Luke 6:27-36

- **Teaching on Prayer**
  Matt 6:5-15 / Matt 7:7-11 / Luke 11:1-13

- **The Lord's Prayer**
  Matt 6:9-15 / Luke 11:2-4

- **Do Not Worry / Treasures in Heaven**
  Matt 6:25-34 / Matt 6:19-21 / Luke 12:22-34

- **Ask, Seek, Knock**
  Matt 7:7-12 / Luke 11:9-13

- **THE GOLDEN RULE**
  Matt 7:12 / Luke 6:31

- **Followers of Christ**
  Matt 8:18-22 / Luke 9:57-62

- **Fasting**
  Matt 9:14-17 / Mark 2:18-22 / Luke 5:33-39

- **Discipleship**
  Matt 10:37-38 / Mark 9:41 / Luke 14:26-33 /
  Matt 10:40-42 / Matt 16:24-28 /

- **Disciples and Spiritual Authority**
  Matt 10:1-15 / Mark 3:13-19 / Mark 6:7-13 /
  Luke 6:12-16 / Luke 9:1-6

- **The Kingdom of God**
  Matt 11:12-13 / Luke 16:14-17

- **The Authority of The Son**
  John 5:19-29

- **Resting in Jesus ('Come to Me all who are weary')**
  Matt 11:25-30

- **Traditions of Men**
  Matt 15:1-20 / Mark 7:1-13

- **Words of Eternal Life**
  John 6:60-71

- **An Adulterous Woman is Forgiven**
  John 8:3-11

- **Jesus, The Light of The World**
  John 8:12-20 / John 9:1-12

- **Jesus, The 'Christ' (The Anointed One)**
  Matt 16:13-20 / Mark 8:27-30 / Luke 9:18-21

- **Jesus predicts His Death and Resurrection**
  Matt 16:21-28 / Mark 8:31-9:1 / Luke 9:22-27
  Matt 17:22-23 / Mark 9:30-32 / Luke 9:43-45
  Matt 20:17-19 / Mark 10:32-34 / Luke 18:31-33

- **Jesus Existed Before Creation**
  John 1:1-5 / John 1:14+18 / John 8:48-59

- **The Transfiguration**
  Matt 17:1-13 / Mark 9:2-13 / Luke 9:28-36

- **The Greatest in The Kingdom of Heaven**
  Matt 18:1-4 / Mark 9:33-35 / Luke 9:46-48 / Luke 22:24-30

- **Do Not Deliberately Offend Others / Avoid Taking Offence**
  Matt 18:6-7 / Mark 9:42 / Luke 17:1-4

- **Jesus Rejoices**
  Luke 10:21-24

- **Knowing God**
  John 14:7-14

- **Marriage**
  Matt 19:1-12 / Mark 10:2-9 / Matt 22:23-33

- **Do Not Reject Children**
  Matt 19:13-15 / Mark 10:13-16 / Luke 18:15-17

- **The Rich Young Ruler**
  Matt 19:16-30 / Mark 10:17-31 / Luke 18:18-30

- **The Widow's Mite**
  Mark 12:41-44 / Luke 21:1-4

- **Jesus, The Resurrection and The Life**
  John 11:18-27

- **Jesus Will Be Lifted Up**
  John 12:27-36

- **Jesus, The Servant (washing the disciples' feet)**
  John 13:1-20

- **A New Commandment (Love one another)**
  John 13:31-35

- **Jesus: The Way, The Truth and The Life**
  John 14:1-6

- **THE GREATEST COMMANDMENT**
  Matt 22:34-40 / Mark 12:28-34 / Luke 10:25-28

- **The Promise of The Holy Spirit**
  John 14:1-14 / John 16:7-15

- **Sorrow will Turn to Joy**
  John 16:16-24

- **Take Heart, Jesus Has Overcome All Things**
  John 16:25-33

- **The Prayer of Jesus**
  John 17:1-26

- **The Coming of God's Kingdom**
  Matt 24:23-28 / Matt 24:37-41/ Luke 17:20-37

- **Prophesy of The Temple Being Destroyed**
  Matt 24:1-2 / Mark 13:1-2 / Luke 21:5-6 / Luke 21:20-24

- **The Last Days**
  Matt 24:3-14 / Mark 13:3-31 / Luke 21:7-19

- **Be Watchful**
  Matt 24:15-44 / Mark 13:32-37 /
  Luke 12:35-40 / Luke 21:34-38

- **Christ's Return**
  Matt 24:29-31 / Mark 13:24-27 / Luke 21:25-28

Section Four

Healings & Miracles

In John's Gospel we are told that Jesus performed many more healings and miracles than have been recorded. In fact, even if the whole world was filled with books, they could never truly explain the magnitude of all Jesus did and said *(John 21:25 / John 20:31)*.

However, the apostle John goes on to say that the purpose of the things that are written down for us, is to show that Jesus was (is) The Messiah sent by God (for the whole world), so that people all over the world may believe.

The Bible's fundamental message is to show all mankind's need for a Saviour (this is particularly seen when reading the Old Testament) ~ leading us to the **Good News** (particularly seen in The New Testament) ~ that God HAS sent His Son, to be the Saviour of all who will put their trust in Him.

> *Taken from John 6:29+38 (GNT) Jesus said....*
> *"What God wants you to do is to believe in The One He sent.... I came down from heaven not to do My own will but the will of Him who sent Me".*

> *Taken from Rom 15:4 (NIV) / 2 Thess 3:5 (GNT)*
> *Everything that was written in the past was written to teach us, so that through the endurance taught in the Scriptures and the encouragement they provide we might have hope..... May the Lord lead you into a greater understanding of God's Love and the endurance that is given by Christ.*

EXAMPLES OF HEALINGS AND MIRACLES OF JESUS
(with Bible references for further study)

- **Turning Water into Wine (Wedding at Cana)**
  John 2:1-11

- **Healing at the Synagogue (in Capernaum)**
  Mark 1:21-28 / Luke 4:31-37

- **Healing of Peter's Mother-in-law**
  Matt 8:14-15 / Mark 1:29-31 / Luke 4:38-39

- **An Evening of Healings**
  Matt 8:16-17 / Mark 1:32-34 / Luke 4:40-41

- **Miraculous Catch of Fish**
  Luke 5:1-11

- **Healing of a Leper**
  Matt 8:1-4 / Mark 1:40-45 / Luke 5:12-16

- **Healing of a Centurion's Servant**
  Matt 8:5-13 / Luke 7:1-10 / John 4:43-54

- **Widow's Son is Raised from The Dead**
  Luke 7:11-17

- **Multitude of People Healed**
  Matt 8:14-17 / Mark 1:29-34 / Luke 4:38-41

- **The Stilling of The Storm**
  Matt 8:23-27 / Mark 4:36-41 / Luke 8:22-25

- **Healing of Demoniacs at Gadarene**
  Matt 8:28-34 / Mark 5:1-20 / Luke 8:26-39

- **Healing of a Paralyzed Man**
  Matt 9:1-8 / Mark 2:1-12 / Luke 5:17-26

- **Healing of Jairus' Daughter**
  Matt 9:18-19+23-26 / Mark 5:21-24+35-43 /
  Luke 8:41-42+49-56

- **The Woman who touched Jesus' Cloak**
  Matt 9:20-23 / Mark 5:25-34 / Luke 8:43-48

- **Healing of Two Men (who couldn't see)**
  Matt 9:27-31

- **Healing of a Man (who couldn't speak)**
  Matt 9:32-33

- **The Compassion of Jesus**
  Matt 9:35-38

- **Healing at The Pool**
  John 5:2-18

- **Healing of a withered hand**
  Matt 12:9-14 / Mark 3:1-6 / Luke 6:6-11

- **God's Chosen Servant (and Healer)**
  Matt 12:15-21

- **A Multitude at the Seaside**
  Mark 3:7-12

- **The Servant from Capernaum**
  Luke 7:1-10

- **A Sinful Woman is Shown Forgiveness**
  Luke 7:36-50

- **The Feeding of The Five Thousand**
  Matt 14:13-21 / Mark 6:30-44 / Luke 9:10-17 / John 6:1-13

- **Walking on Water**
  Matt 14:22-33 / Mark 6:45-51

- **Healings at Gennesaret**
  Matt 14:34-36 / Mark 6:53-56

- **The Syrophoenician Woman**
  Matt 15:21-28 / Mark 7:24-30

- **Healing of a Man (who could not speak nor hear)**
  Mark 7:32-37

- **Healing of Many People**
  Matt 15:29-31

- **The Feeding of The Four Thousand**
  Matt 15:32-39 / Mark 8:1-9

- **Healing of a Man Born Blind**
  John 9:1-12

- **Healing of a Blind Man at Bethsaida**
  Mark 8:22-26

- **Healing of an Epileptic Child**
  Matt 17:14-18 / Mark 9:14-27 / Luke 9:38-42

- **Healing of a Woman on The Sabbath**
  Luke 13:10-17

- **Healing of a Man (with dropsy)**
  Luke 14:1-4

- **The Healing of Ten Lepers**
  Luke 17:11-19

- **Lazarus is Raised from The Dead**
  John 11:38-46

- **Blind Men receive their Sight**
  Matt 20:29-34 / Mark 10:46-52 / Luke 18:35-43

- **A Voice Speaks from Heaven**
  John 12:27-30

- **Jesus heals a Servant's Ear**
  Luke 22:47-53

SOME THOUGHTS TO CONSIDER:

In The Old Testament, there were many prophesies about The Promised Saviour (The Messiah). Many spoke about how He would save people from their sins, and bring healing and wholeness to people's lives.

For example:

Isaiah 53:5 (GNT)
...Because of our sins He was wounded, beaten because of the evil we did. We are healed by the punishment He suffered, made whole by the blows He received.

When He was on earth, Jesus healed all who came to Him. He forgave sins and set people free from spiritual bondage. He healed through the supernatural power of God and through His Spoken Word.

His healing work is still producing results in people's lives today. But it is important to realise that God will use both natural and supernatural ways to help us. The main point is to look to Him for our healing and to receive His forgiveness in our lives.

God's will is always to heal and He wants to give us good things. Sometimes healing can take forms we don't understand or is progressive. But we can trust God's Son [through whom all things were created] to use the best means for our welfare in each situation.

The Bible includes examples of medicine being used to help people. There is a 'Balm of Gilead' mentioned in Old Testament Scriptures (for example in Genesis 37:25).

The Bible also tell us to speak good words over our own lives and the lives of others, for kind words can also release healing into our souls and bodies.

> *Proverbs 16:24 (NLT)*
> *Kind words are like honey—sweet to the soul and healthy for the body.*
>
> *Proverbs 12:18 (MSG)*
> *Rash language cuts and maims, but there is healing in the words of the wise.*

Ultimately, Jesus is our Healer; He is the greatest 'Balm of Gilead' and the greatest 'Word of Kindness' that can be spoken over our lives.

The greatest healing of all is found at The Cross, where Jesus paid for all sin, for all time.

We simply receive His Sacrifice of Love that has healing power to go deep into our very soul and produce eternal life that begins in our hearts the moment put our trust in Him.

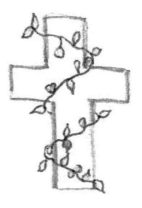

Section Five

The Cross

Jesus goes to Jerusalem for The Passover Festival

When Jesus was 33 years old, He journeyed once again to Jerusalem for the Passover Festival. As they neared the city, Jesus sent His disciples ahead of Him to make preparation for them all to celebrate The Passover Meal together.

He told His disciples that they would find a colt (a young donkey) tied up, that had never been ridden. He told them to ask its owner for use of the animal, saying "our Master has need of the donkey".

They went, found everything just as He said it would be, and the owner released the animal to them. Jesus climbed on the back of the colt without it being at all troubled by the new experience.

As He entered Jerusalem, riding the donkey, the people welcomed Him with loud cheers. They threw coats and palm branches along His path as a sign of honour to Him. The people greeted Him with cries of praise, saying "Hosanna, blessed is He who comes in the name of The Lord".

> *Zechariah 9:9 (NLT)*
> **A prophesy about The Messiah in Old Testament**
> *Rejoice, O people of Zion! Shout in triumph, O people of Jerusalem! Look, your king is coming to you. He is righteous and victorious, yet He is humble, riding on a donkey— riding on a donkey's colt.*

However, the people expected Jesus to deliver them from The Roman Army (who occupied the land at that time). They were looking for a political solution to their situation.

Yet, Jesus had repeatedly taught that His deliverance was to free people from sin, and that His Kingdom was an Eternal Kingdom which came from Heaven itself.

Jesus had displayed the freedom of His Kingdom in signs and wonders everywhere He taught. He had taught that the right way to live was to worship God and to honour oneanother with love and respect.

But the people were still looking for political freedom more than spiritual. Then, when Jesus went into The Temple, He saw that there were sellers and money changers there who were hindering the purpose of The Temple and exploiting the people.

In His indignation, He drove out all who were misusing the area and told them: "My House is a House of Prayer, but you have turned it into a den of thieves!"

The Last Supper

Later, as Jesus and His disciples celebrated The Passover meal together, He used the special meal as symbolism to try and explain the sacrifice that He was about to make for all people everywhere, to pay for all sin. Today we recognise this occasion as 'The Last Supper'.

The meal took place on the first day of Passover (also known as the Festival of Unleavened Bread).

As Jesus and His disciples ate together, He told them that one of them would betray Him, which appalled them all (but soon after the meal Judas did betray Jesus).

Jesus prayed and thanked God for the meal, and then broke the bread and shared the wine among the disciples.

He said that the bread was symbolic of His own body broken for them, and that the wine symbolised His blood which would be shed for them, for the forgiveness of sin.

(Today, churches celebrate 'Communion' in remembrance of Jesus, using the same symbolism as He taught at The Last Supper).

During the meal, Jesus got up and put a towel around His waist and became like a servant, then washed His disciples' feet.

He used this to teach them that He had come to serve (even though He is The King of Heaven) and as an example to them to also serve one another. At first, Peter struggled to allow Jesus to serve him, but Jesus explained the importance of this act, and so Peter agreed.

The Garden of Gethsemane

After Jesus and His Disciples had celebrated The Passover Meal, they went on to pray at the 'Garden of Gethsemane'.

(The name means 'oil press' and this garden of olive trees can be still be found today, situated on an incline at the Mount of Olives).

Jesus took Peter, James and John with Him. Jesus asked them to 'keep watch' and pray that they would not fall into temptation. However, the disciples were tired and fell asleep. Twice Jesus came to them to wake them and asked them again to pray.

Jesus went to pray alone for a time, and asked His Heavenly Father to 'remove the cup' that He was about to drink from.

By this He meant the cup of suffering that He was about to endure at The Cross. However, Jesus also said to His Father "but not My Will be done but Yours".

Jesus was deeply distressed; His anguish was so great that He even sweated drops of blood. So His Father sent an angel to strengthen Him. Again, Jesus submitted Himself to His Father's Will, as The Father reminded Him that there was no other way to save mankind.

Meanwhile, Judas Iscariot arrived with a great number of soldiers (as well as some of The Religious Leaders and their servants) who had come to arrest Jesus.

This multitude arrived with lanterns, torches and weapons. Judas approached Jesus and kissed Him as a signal to the crowd to come and make the arrest.

On seeing this, Peter rose to defend Jesus. Peter attacked a man named 'Malchus' (who was a servant of The High Priest). But Jesus rebuked Peter and miraculously healed the servant's ear that Peter had cut off.

When Jesus was asked 'are you Jesus of Nazareth?' He replied saying "I AM", and He spoke with such power that the crowd fell to the ground.

Despite this incredible display of power, Jesus allowed Himself to be arrested and taken to Pontius Pilate, while the disciples scattered in fear.

This part of His Story shows the commitment of Jesus towards you and I, that He went willingly to The Cross to pay for the sins of The World. He went there for you and I.

At The Cross and in His sorrow in the garden, Jesus identified with every pain and suffering you and I have ever known. He experienced it all and ultimately overcame it. In Him we now can find strength.

Jesus Trial

The religious leaders who hated Jesus accused Him of 'blasphemy' because they wanted to pass a death sentence on Him. So they questioned Him intensely and beat Him.

But they needed approval of the Roman authorities, so Jesus was taken for trial before Pontius Pilate (the Roman Governor in Judea).

Pilate questioned Jesus but concluded that He was innocent. However, Pilate feared the crowd that had been stirred up by the religious leaders against Jesus, so Pilate chose to let the people decide what would happen to Jesus.

Once again, stirred up and influenced by the hatred of some of the religious leaders, the crowd shouted out their answer "Crucify Him".

So, Jesus was publicly beaten with a whip. He was also struck with a staff, spat on and mocked. As part of the mockery and torment, a crown of thorns was placed upon His head.

After all the beating, Jesus became too weak to carry His cross and so a man named Simon of Cyrene was made to carry it for Him.

Jesus was led outside the walls of Jerusalem to a place named 'Golgotha' (Calvary), where He was crucified. An inscription was placed above Jesus head which read: 'The King of The Jews'.

The Cross

The Cross of Jesus stood between two thieves who were also being crucified that day.

One thief hung on a cross on His left, and the other on His right. One mocked Jesus, just as the crowd did.

But the other rebuked his fellow criminal's insults, saying that they were both guilty of their crime, but that Jesus was innocent.

With that, He turned to Jesus in repentance. Jesus replied to him that he would be with Jesus in 'paradise' that same day.

Jesus hung on The Cross for six hours. During that time, soldiers gambled for His clothing, while passersby hurled insults and abuse at Him. From The Cross He gave His mother Mary into the future care of His disciple John.

On The Cross, Jesus identified with the pain of all mankind. Then, just before He died, Jesus shouted out in anguish, "My God, My God, why have You forsaken Me?"

As He died the land was covered in darkness, and an earthquake shook the ground. The Temple veil (that separated the Most Holy Place) was torn in two from top to bottom.

As the earth shook, rocks split open, and tombs broke open. Many holy people who had died were raised up to life (who were later seen in the towns after Jesus' resurrection).

It was the usual practice for Roman soldiers to break the legs of those being crucified to hasten death.

However when they came to Jesus they found that He had already died and therefore did not carry out their custom *(this was prophesied in Psalm 22 in the Old Testament).*

Instead they pierced His side, and blood and water poured out *(which is medically understood to mean the person had died).*

Before the sun set that day, Nicodemus and Joseph of Arimathea took down the body of Jesus and laid Him in Joseph's tomb.

SOME THOUGHTS TO CONSIDER:

The significance of the curtain being torn in two (from top to bottom) is that, in Jewish tradition, only The High Priest was able to enter into the Most Holy Place. Once a year, The High priest would do so in order to make an offering for the sins of the people.

When the curtain tore at the time of Jesus' death (being torn from heaven to earth) it symbolized that the barrier between God and man had now been removed. It shows that Christ's sacrifice has opened the way for each one of us to know God as He truly is, and that we can approach His Throne of Grace through His Son.

Hebrews 4:16 (NIV)
Let us then approach God's throne of grace with confidence, so that we may receive mercy and find grace to help us in our time of need.

RELATED BIBLE REFERENCES
FOR SOME KEY POINTS IN THIS PART OF HIS STORY

Jesus Travels to Jerusalem and enters
The City Riding on a Young Donkey (a colt)
Matt 21:1-11 / Mark 11:1-11 /
Luke 19:28-38 / John 12:1-19

Jesus Cleanses The Temple
Matt 21:12-17 / Mark 11:15-19 /
Luke 19:45-48 / John 2:13-22

The Plot to Kill Jesus
Matt 26:1-5 / Mark 14:1-2 /
Luke 22:1-2 / John 11:46-57

Judas Betrays Jesus *(for thirty pieces of silver ~ the price of a slave)*
Matt 26:14-16 / Mark 14:10-11 /
Luke 22:3-6 / John 18:1-3

The Last Supper (Passover Meal)
Matt 26:17-30 / Mark 14:12-26 /
Luke 22:7-23 / John 13:1-30

Garden of Gethsemane
Matt 26:30+36-46 / Mark 14:26+32-42 /
Luke 22:39-46 / John 18:1

The Arrest of Jesus
Matt 26:47-56 / Mark 14:43-50 /
Luke 22:47-53 / John 18:3-12

Jesus Questioned and Put on Trial
Matt 26:57-68 / Matt 27:1-2+11-14 / Mark 14:53-65 /
Mark 15:1-5 / Luke 22:54-55+63-71 / Luke 23:1-12 /
John 18:13-14+19-24+28-38

Peter Denies Knowing Jesus
Matt 26:69-75 / Mark 14:66-72 /
Luke 22:56-62 / John 18:15-18+25-27

Jesus is Sentenced
Matt 27:15-26 / Mark 15:6-15 / Luke 23:13-25 /
John 18:28 to John 19:16

Jesus is Mocked and Beaten *(before and after sentencing)*
Matt 26:67-68 / Matt 27:27-31 / Mark 14:65 /
Mark 15:16-20 / Luke 22:63-65 / John 19:2-3

Judas dies
Matt 27:3-10

The Cross
Matt 27:32-56 / Mark 15:21-41 /
Luke 23:26-49 / John 19:16-37

Jesus' Burial
Matt 27:57-61 / Mark 15:42-47 /
Luke 23:50-56 / John 19:38-42

A Guard is Placed at The Tomb
Matt 27:62-66

Section Six

Jesus is Alive!

The Empty Tomb

There were many women who were followers of Jesus, who had spent much of their time supporting Him and His disciples in their work.

Some of these women, along with Mary Magdalene (whom Jesus had healed during His ministry) had prepared spices for Jesus' burial.

So, early on the Sunday morning (the day following the Sabbath) they went to the tomb with their spices. However, when they arrived, they found that the huge stone (that had been sealed around the tomb) had been rolled away.

They looked inside for Jesus' body but could not find Him. Suddenly two angels appeared in dazzling white clothing. The women were frightened, but the angels spoke and reassured them saying,

"Why do you look for the living among the dead? He is not here; He has risen! Remember how He told you that He would be handed over to sinful men, crucified, and rise up on the third day!"

In excitement, the women ran back to tell the disciples what they had seen. Peter and John ran to the tomb to see for themselves.

When they looked inside, they saw the linen cloths that Jesus' body had been wrapped in, but no body, and so went home, stunned and confused.

Jesus Appears to Mary Magdalene

When Peter and John went home, Mary Magdalene stayed at the tomb crying. Through her tears, she suddenly saw Jesus standing there but did not recognise Him. Jesus spoke to her saying, "Woman, why are you crying? Who are you looking for?"

Mary assumed the man talking to her must be the gardener, so she replied "sir, if you have taken Him away, please tell me where He is". But Jesus simply spoke her name; suddenly she recognised Him and cried out "Master!".

He then told her that He had not yet returned to The Father but said 'I AM ascending to My Father and your Father; to My God and your God".

After this encounter, Mary ran to meet the disciples and shouted to them, "I have seen The Lord!". She then told them everything that had happened.

Jesus talks with Two Disciples on the Road to Emmaus

Later that day, two disciples of Jesus were walking along a road towards a village called Emmaus. They were talking and pondering over all the things that had happened.

Suddenly Jesus appeared beside them and was walking with them. But they did not recognise Him. Jesus asked the disciples, "what are you talking about?" to which they replied in astonishment, "are you the only one in Jerusalem that doesn't know the things that have been happening these past few days?"

So, Jesus asked them to tell Him. They began telling Him that they believed in Jesus of Nazareth, and that He was a prophet before God and all the people.

They said that they had hoped He would redeem Israel, but the Religious Leaders had handed Him over to the ruling authorities of the land to be crucified.

They went on to explain that women from their group had gone to the tomb but could not find Jesus' body there. Instead they had seen angels who told the women He had risen from the dead!

Having listen to the disciples, Jesus replied to them saying, "Wasn't it necessary for The Christ to suffer these things and enter into His Glory?"

Later, when Jesus was eating with them, He blessed the bread and broke it, and gave it to His disciples. Suddenly they recognised Him, and He vanished from their sight.

After this, the two disciples quickly returned to Jerusalem to find the eleven apostles, and others who followed Jesus, to tell the group that He had appeared to them.

Jesus Appears to the Rest of The Disciples

On the same Sunday evening, many of the disciples were hiding in a locked room together, in fear that the religious authorities may want to kill them next.

But Jesus appeared among them and said: "Peace be with you".

On this occasion, Thomas was not with them. On hearing what had happened, he doubted and insisted that he would not believe unless he saw the nail holes in Jesus hands and put his own hand in the wound on Jesus side.

However, a week later, when the disciples were together again in the same room (and Thomas was with them) Jesus appeared and stood among them all. He said to Thomas "Look at My Hands and put your hand in My Side. Don't doubt. Believe!"

Thomas said, "my Lord and my God!" Then Jesus said to him, "Do you believe because you have seen? Blessed are those who have not seen and yet believe."

Jesus' Instructions to His disciples

Jesus spoke to His disciples saying:
"All authority in heaven and on earth has been given to Me. Therefore, go and make disciples of all nations, baptizing them in the name of The Father, The Son and The Holy Spirit, and teaching them everything I have commanded you. And surely, I AM with you always, to the very end of the age."
(Taken from Matthew 28:18-20 NIV)

Jesus Ascends to Heaven

After Jesus resurrection, He stayed on earth for 40 days and appeared again to the disciples at the Sea of Galilee (also known as The Sea of Tiberias). He also appeared to them on a mountainside in Galilee and to another 500 people across the region.

When it was time for Jesus to return to heaven, He took His disciples to a place near Bethany (on the slopes of the Mount of Olives). Jesus blessed them and ascended to heaven, as the disciples watched until they lost sight of Him in a cloud.

From Acts 1:3 / 1 Cor 15:6 / Acts 1:9-11 (NLT)
During the forty days after He suffered and died, He appeared to the apostles from time to time, and He proved to them in many ways that He was actually alive. And He talked to them about the Kingdom of God... After that, He was seen by more than 500 of His followers at one time... After (speaking to His disciples), He was taken up into a cloud while they were watching, and they could no longer see Him. As they strained to see Him rising into heaven, two white-robed men suddenly stood among them. "Men of Galilee," they said, "why are you standing here staring into heaven? .... someday He will return from heaven in the same way you saw Him go!"

RELATED BIBLE REFERENCES
FOR SOME KEY POINTS IN THIS PART OF HIS STORY

The Resurrection
Matt 28:1-10 / Mark16:1-8 /
Luke 24:1-12 / John 20:1-10

Jesus Appears to Mary
Matt 28:1-10 / Mark 16:9-11 / John 20:11-18

The Guards are Bribed *(to give a false report)*
Matt 28:11-15

Jesus' Appearance on The Road to Emmaus
Mark 16:12-13 / Luke 24:13-35

Jesus' Appears to The Disciples
Mark 16:14-18 / Luke 24:36-49 /
John 20:19-23 / John 21:1-14

Jesus and Thomas
John 20:24-29

Jesus shows His Forgiveness to Peter
John 21:15-19

Jesus and John
John 21:20-25

The Great Commission
Matt 28:16-20

The Ascension of Christ
Mark 16:19-20 / Luke 24:50-53

SOME THOUGHTS TO CONSIDER:

The Old Testament (O.T.) shares many prophesies and predictions about the ***Promised Saviour (The Messiah)*** that God promised to send. So, for further consideration, below are some O.T. predictions along with Bible references to compare with related New Testament (N.T.) references.

Some of the N.T. references are taken from The Gospels, while others are from The Book of Acts (which follows The Gospels in The Bible) and others are from some of The Letters written by The Apostles (which were written to teach and encourage the growing church).

There are many more prophesies to be found in the Scriptures but here are some examples for personal reflection and further study (if desired):

1. THE MESSIAH WOULD BE BORN OF A VIRGIN
Compare (O.T.) Isaiah 7:14 with
(N.T.) Matt 1:22-23 / Luke 1:31-35

2. HE WOULD BE BORN IN BETHLEHEM
Compare (O.T.) Micah 5:2 with
(N.T.) Matt 2:1-6 / John 7:40-43

3. HE WOULD BE CALLED OUT OF EGYPT
Compare (O.T.) Hosea 11:1 with
(N.T.) Matthew 2:13-15

4. HE WOULD BE PRECEDED BY A MESSENGER
(one like Elijah the prophet)
Compare (O.T.) Malachi 3:1+ Malachi 4:5-6 with
(N.T.) Matt 11:10+14-15 / Matt 16:14+17:9-13 /
Mark 1:1-2+6:14-16+9:11-13 / Luke 1:16-17+76 / John 1:21

5. HE WOULD PERFORM HEALINGS AND MIRACLES
(by The Power of God's Spirit)
Compare (O.T.) Isaiah 35:5-6 and Isaiah 61:1-2 with
(N.T.) Matt 11:4-6 / Luke 4:17-21+7:20-23

6. HE WOULD BE CALLED GOD'S SON
Compare (O.T.) Psalm 2:1-12 with
(N.T.) Mark 1:11 / Luke 3:22 /
Acts 4:25-28 / Hebrews 1:5+5:5

7. HE WOULD BE CALLED SON OF MAN
Compare (O.T.) Daniel 7:13-14 with
(N.T.) Matt 9:6+12:8+13:41+16:13+27 / Mark 8:31 /
Luke 6:22+9:22 / John 1:51+3:13-14 / Acts 7:56

8. HE WOULD BE A LIGHT FOR ALL NATIONS
Compare (O.T.) Isaiah 42:1-7 with
(N.T.) Matt 12:15-18 / Luke 2:27-32 / John 8:12

9. HE WOULD APPEAR RIDING ON A DONKEY'S COLT
Compare (O.T.) Zechariah 9:9 with (N.T.) Matthew 21:1-7

10. HE WOULD BRING IN A NEW COVENANT
Compare (O.T.) Jeremiah 31:31 with
(N.T.) Matt 26:26-28 / Mark 14:24 / Luke 22:20 /
1 Corinthians 11:25 / 2 Corinthians 3:6 /
Hebrews 8:6-13+9:15+12:24

11. HE WOULD BE A SUFFERING SERVANT
Compare (O.T.) Isaiah 52:13 to Isaiah 53:12 with
(N.T.) Matt 8:16-17+20:28+26:28+27:59-60 / Mark 10:45
Mark 14:24 / Luke 22:20 / John 12:37-38 / Acts 8:32-35 /
Romans 10:16 / Hebrews 9:28 / 1 Peter 2:21-25

12. HE WOULD BE BETRAYED FOR 30 PIECES OF SILVER
Compare (O.T.) Zechariah 11:12-13 with
(N.T.) Matt 26:14-15+27:3+9-10

13. HE WOULD BE FORSAKEN AND PIERCED, BUT WOULD BE VINDICATED
Compare (O.T.) Psalm 22:1-31 with
(N.T.) Matt 27:39-46 / Mark 15:34
/ John 19:24 / Hebrews 2:12

14. HE WOULD BE A WILLING SACRIFICE
Compare (O.T.) Genesis 22:1-18 with
(N.T.) John 3:16 / Hebrews 11:17-19

15. HE WOULD RISE FROM THE DEAD
Compare (O.T.) Psalm 16:8-11 with
(N.T.) Acts 2:22-32+13:35-37

16. HE WOULD SIT DOWN AT THE RIGHT HAND OF GOD
(having completed His Mission)
Compare (O.T.) Psalm 110:1 with
(N.T.) Acts 2:33 / Hebrews 1:3

Section Seven

The Holy Spirit

God keeps His Promises

In The Gospels, Jesus promised that after He had returned to heaven, God would send another 'Comforter' or 'Helper.' He promised that His Father would send **The Holy Spirit** to be with us, and in us, always.

> *John 14:16-24*
> *I will ask the Father, and He will give you another Helper to be with you forever— The Spirit of Truth. The world cannot accept Him, because it does not see Him or know Him. But you know Him, because He lives with you and He will be in you. I will not leave you all alone like orphans; I will come back to you. In a little while the world will not see Me anymore, but you will see Me. Because I live, you will live, too. On that day you will know that I AM in My Father, and that you are in Me and I AM in you. ²¹ Those who know My commands and obey them are the ones who love Me, and My Father will love those who love Me. I will love them and will show Myself to them."*

After John's Gospel in The Bible, another Bible Book begins called 'ACTS'. It is here that we see The Holy Spirit, 'poured out at Pentecost' (as God also promised in The Old Testament).

> *Joel 2:28*
> *I will pour out My Spirit upon all people. Your sons and daughters will prophesy. Your old men will dream dreams, and your young men will see visions.*

In ACTS we see the Birth of The Church and the promise of the sending of The Holy Spirit fulfilled. And He is still at work in people's lives today.

Jesus said that The Holy Spirit would lead us into all truth, and that He would take the things that Jesus had spoken and speak them to our hearts and help us to understand more about Jesus' Teaching, if we ask Him in faith.

The Holy Spirit is at work all around the world today speaking to people's hearts, if they will listen. But He will always honour God's Word (The Bible is God's written Word / Jesus is God's Living Word).

For further study, some more references to THE HOLY SPIRIT found in THE GOSPELS ~ Matt 28:19-20 / Mark 1:9-11 / Luke 1:30-35 / Luke 12:12 / John 1:32-34 / John 3:5 / John 7:37-39 / John 14:16-17 / John 14:26-27 / John 16:7-8 / John 16:13-15 / John 20:21-23

For further study, some more references to THE HOLY SPIRIT found in ACTS ~ Acts 2:1-4 / Acts 2:33 / Acts 8:29 / Acts 10:19-20 / Acts 13:2

For further study, some more references to THE HOLY SPIRIT found in the NEW TESTAMENT LETTERS (written by The Apostles) ~ Rom 8:11 / 1 Cor 6:19 / 1 Cor 12:7-11 / 2 Cor 1:21-22 / Gal 5:22-25 / 2 Peter 1:20-21

The Holy Spirit is even at work in people before they really know much about God, prompting them to ask questions about life, God and eternity.

We do not earn salvation; it is a GIFT of God's Grace. He simply wants us to receive His great gift and learn from Him.

When we receive Jesus into our hearts, The Holy Spirit helps us to grow spiritually and develop a deeper relationship with our Heavenly Father.

He builds our character, and helps us to learn how to bring God's order to our lives. He will also fill us with ***power to live*** the Christian life if we ask Him.

The Holy Spirit and God's Word will always agree. He will speak in Love and Grace, encouraging us even when He is teaching us a better way to live. As Romans chapter 8, verse 1 tells us: ***In Christ, there is no condemnation.***

Therefore, the best place we can be is 'In Christ' (which simply means we have right standing with God through faith in His Son).

Through Christ, we can receive ALL of God's great and precious promises, which can be found in The Bible.

For example:

- God has promised to lead us and be with us always, and promises that He will never leave nor forsake us (Deut 31:8 / Matt 28:20 / Heb 13:5).

- He has promised good plans for us and that He will turn things around for good (Jer 29:11 / Rom 8:28)

- He has promised that when we welcome Jesus, we welcome God Himself, and He will make His home in our hearts (Matt 10:40 / Luke 9:48 / John 13:20 / Rev 3:20).

- He has promised that all who receive Jesus become God's Children ~ God becomes our Father! (John 1:12 / Rom 8:15-16 / 1 John 3:1).

- He has promised to forgive us of all sin, as we confess them to God, through His Son (1 John 1:9 / Eph 1:7 / Heb 10:12-14).

- He has promised to give The Holy Spirit to all who ask Him (Luke 11:13 / John 14:16-17 / John 15:26).

- He has promised to pour out His Love and the Holy Spirit into our hearts (Rom 5:5 / Is 44:3 / Acts 2:1-4 / 1 Cor 12:13)

- He has promised to help us and uphold us. And He promises to strengthen us when we feel weak (Is 40:29+31 / Is 41:10 / 2 Cor 12:9).

- He has promised to make us a 'New Creation' in Christ and to give us a new heart in Him (2 Cor 5:17 / John 3:3 / Is 43:19 / Ex 36:26 / Gal 6:15).

- He has promised to produce good things in us, including the presence of love, peace, joy, patience, kindness, goodness, faithfulness, gentleness and self-control within our hearts (which is 'fruit of The Holy Spirit' as shown in Gal 5:22-23)

Here are some more examples of God's Promises
PERSONALISED

(all are taken from The Bible, and included in the book called 'PROMISES ~ Messages from God's Heart to yours')

Eternal life is to know My Son Jesus ~ The One who came down from Heaven to reveal the true nature of My heart. In Him alone is eternal hope and salvation. *(John 17:3 / John 1: 18 / Rom 10:13)*

Everyone who hears My Word of Life and believes in His Name passes from death to life ~ for Jesus came to give you real life in all its abundance, here and now, and for all eternity. *(John 5:24 / John 10:10 / 1 John 2:25)*

No one can snatch you from My hand of love and forgiveness when you put your faith in Christ. For I sent Him not to condemn the world but to save it. *(John 10:28 / Acts 2:38-39 / John 3:17)*

My promise of eternal life is to all who come to Me through Him, and I promise to remain with you for all time, because I have made My home within your heart. *(Eph 2:8-9 / Heb 13:5 / John 14:23)*

PERSONAL STUDY NOTES

About The Author
And Gardenland Ministries

About the Author and 'Gardenland'

John and Carmel have an online resource of Bible Studies and Teaching Letters to offer encouragement, and share the Good News of God's unconditional love for people, whoever they are, wherever they maybe. Carmel first began to write books in 2012 when they lived in Bedford UK.

Since moving to North Derbyshire in 2018, they continue to provide free online resources on their websites and social media (please see below) and Carmel continues to write books that can be found at Amazon across the world.

GLM's foundational Scriptures: Isaiah 58:11 & Psalm 96:3 say:

"The LORD will guide you always; He will give you water when you are dry and restore your strength. You will be like a well-watered garden, like an ever-flowing spring... Publish His glorious deeds among the nations. Tell everyone about the amazing things God does!"

For more encouragement please see websites and social media links:

www.gardenlandministries.org
https://carmelcarberry.wordpress.com
www.facebook.com/groups/gardenlandministries
https://www.facebook.com/CarmelCarberry - Author
https://twitter.com/CarmelCarberry
https://www.instagram.com/carmelcarberry/

Books by the author (find at Amazon)

<u>THE HIS STORY BOOK SERIES</u>

His Story Volume 1 ~ looking at GENESIS

His Story Volume 2 ~ looking at THE GOSPELS

His Story Volume 3 ~ looking at ACTS and the New Testament Letters

---

<u>GARDENLAND BOOKS</u>

God's Fruitful Garden (a book of hope and encouragement)

Communion With God (Soaring on Eagles Wings)

SonRise (Heaven Scent)

SonSet (On The Throne)

SonDown (a taste of Heaven on Earth) ~ includes Bible Studies

Promises (Messages from God's Heart to yours)

Prayers and Blessings (Help in times of need)

Contrast (looks at Bible Covenants and the 'NEW YOU' in Christ)

Our Identity In Christ (a fresh look at our identity in Him)

Any Year Diary (with colour pictures and Bible verses)

Encouragement Notebook (notetaking journal with messages of hope)

<u>THE ABI TAILS BOOKS SERIES</u>

Funny stories about the family dog 'Abi' ~ with puppy pictures in full colour ~ for all ages

Abi Tails Volume 1 ~ Training my humans

Abi Tails Volume 2 ~ New Adventures

Our Beliefs at Gardenland Ministries

We believe in the authority of Scripture and that Jesus is The Living Word of God (2 Tim 3:16-17 / John 1:1+18 / Heb 1:3)

We believe in Father, Son, and Holy Spirit ~ One God manifest in three persons (Matt 28:18-19 / 2 Cor 13:14)

We believe in the death, burial and resurrection of Christ, who is now seated in Heaven at the right hand of God (1 Cor 15:3-8 / Mark 16:19-20)

We believe that anyone who puts his/her trust in Jesus is born again and becomes a new creation (Rom 10:9-13 / Rom 3:22 / 2 Cor 5:17)

We believe in the Love and Grace of God, who is full of mercy and compassion to all who come to Him (Psalm 145:8 / Eph 2:4 / Rom 8:1)

We believe in the finished work of Jesus at The Cross and that He paid for all sin for all time (Heb 7:24-25 / Rom 8:34 / Heb 4:16)

We believe that salvation includes healing (Is 53:4-5 / Luke 4:18-19 / 1 Peter 2:24)

We believe that The Holy Spirit fills and empowers believers with supernatural gifts and abilities to do good (Acts 1:8+2:4 / 1 Cor 12:7)

We believe that The Body of Christ spans across all nations and all time, united by God's eternal love (Eph 1:22-23 / Rom 12:5 / 1 Cor 12:27 / John 13:35)

YOU MATTER TO GOD

Encouragements and Prayer

A Message from God's Heart

I love you so much that I sent My one and only Son, so that through faith in Him you can receive eternal life. I did not send Him to condemn or punish you, I sent Him to rescue you.

All people everywhere have sinned, but I have demonstrated My Love for all people by sending Jesus to die on The Cross to pay for sin forever.

By faith, you can receive My free gift of salvation, for I have already provided it for you, freely by My Grace, and now you simply receive it by putting your trust in Jesus.

When you receive My Son into your heart, a spiritual new birth happens within you ~ you become My Dearly Beloved Child forever, and you become a New Creation!

As you continue to look to My Son day by day, My Holy Spirit will teach and guide you, and I will rejoice over you with singing!

With Eternal Love & Blessing
From your Heavenly Father

Related Bible verses: John 3:16-17 / Rom 3:22-24+5:8 / Eph 2:8 / John 1:12 / 2 Cor 5:17 / John 16:13 / Zeph 3:17

Please say this prayer from your heart if you would like to make Jesus Lord and Saviour of your life.....

PRAYER

Dear Lord Jesus,

Thank You that You have always loved me.

I admit that I have lived my life for myself. I am sorry and repent of my sin.

Thank You that You died on The Cross to save me. I receive the forgiveness that You earned for me.

I believe that You rose from the dead and are now seated at the right hand of The Father.

Please come into my heart to be my Lord and Saviour. Thank You that the moment I asked, You came in, to be with me forever!

Please fill me with Your Holy Spirit and empower me with good gifts to help others. To the honour of Your Name.

Amen

Welcome to the family of God!

John 1:12 (Taken from the Amplified Bible)
All who receive and welcome Him, He gives the right
[the authority, the privilege] to become children of God,
that is, to those who believe in (adhere to, trust in,
and rely on) His name

When you trust in Jesus, The Bible says these things about you....

...you are a new creation (2 Cor 5:17) you are blessed (Eph 1:3) you are God's child (John 1:12) you are redeemed (Eph 1:7-8) you are included in God's eternal plan (Eph 1:13) you have His strength and power living within you (Eph 1:19-21) you are alive in Christ and filled with God's love (Eph 2:4-6) you are seated in Heavenly places with Jesus, spiritually (Eph 2:6) you are 'hand-made' by God, His work of art (Eph 2:10) you have eternal access to God, without fear or shame (Eph 2:17-18) you are part of God's living temple, where He delights to live (Eph 2:21-22) you share in the promises of Christ as one of His heirs (Eph 3:6) you can approach God with freedom and confidence (Eph 3:12) you are being strengthened by Him in your inner being (Eph 3:16) you are loved much more than you can mentally comprehend (Eph 3:18-19) you have His power at work in you to do more than you can imagine (Eph 3:20) you are being built up and equipped for service (Eph 4:11-13) you have favour with God but He has no favourites, all are loved equally (Eph 6:9) you are strong in The Lord and His mighty power (Eph 6:10) you overcome spiritual darkness though His Light and His Word (Eph 6:12-13) you have His truth, righteousness, peace, faith, salvation, Spirit and Word to enable you (Eph 6:14-17) you have the love and peace of Christ within you, forever and for all time (Eph 6:23).

Enjoy these truths and enjoy your new relationship with God! Please use the free resources and other helpful links that can be found at **www.gardenlandministries.org** *to encourage and bless your journey with Him.*